Polina & the Pomegranate

poems by

Kathryn Kimball

Finishing Line Press
Georgetown, Kentucky

Polina & the Pomegranate

Copyright © 2025 by Kathryn Kimball
ISBN 979-8-88838-877-8 First Edition
All rights reserved under International and Pan-American Copyright Conventions. No part of this book may be reproduced in any manner whatsoever without written permission from the publisher, except in the case of brief quotations embodied in critical articles and reviews.

ACKNOWLEDGMENTS

Acknowledgment of previously published poems: *432 Hz* in *The Dewdrop; Polina & the Pomegranate* in *Tipton Poetry Journal; Wind* in *Atlanta Review.*

Publisher: Leah Huete de Maines
Editor: Christen Kincaid
Cover Art: John Singer Sargent, *Pomegranates, Majorca,* 1908
Author Photo: Andrew Kimball
Cover Design: Elizabeth Maines McCleavy

Order online: www.finishinglinepress.com
also available on amazon.com

Author inquiries and mail orders:
Finishing Line Press
PO Box 1626
Georgetown, Kentucky 40324
USA

Contents

Tears of Gold 1
Desire 2
Daughter of Adam 3
Fig Gathering 4
Anogi 5
Florentine Extravagance 7
Immanence 8
Turquoise is French 9
At Casa Letizia 10
None Too Early 11
Waves 12
To the Tango Shoe 13
The death of the fly 14
Diagnosis for Back Pain 15
Compromised 16
The Middle Way 17
North Truro 18
Here I Am 19
Joan of Arc and the Angels 20
Revisiting Orvieto 21
Polina & the Pomegranate 23
Abridgment 24
Bon Art 25
Private Map 26
Pink Feathers 27
Irish Peat 28
Sitting with the Quakers 29
Harsh Winter 30

In Entire Forgetfulness	31
In-between Time	32
Night Sky	33
The Egyptian Water Lily	35
Galaxies	36
Open Studio	37
Matinee	38
Metaphor	39
No Mind at Howk Waterfall	40
432 Hz	41
To the Poet Offering an Opinion on the Rapture	42
Philip Glass Concert	43
Drumbeat	44
On My Seventieth Birthday	45
Wind	46
On Finding a Deliquescing Mouse in the Bathtub Drain	47
Weight	48
Washing the Dead	49
Elemental Alchemy	50
Seeing the Last	51

For Andrew

*Love grows wild
like red poppies
in a wide field.*

Tears of Gold

The moment before my birth
my mother cried tears of gold.

She paid herself for all the trouble
I had caused
would cause
still causing

though she is dead and
I am still being born.

Desire

I was sixteen
when I first kissed a boy
in the back seat
of a car
and went home
changed by the body's
dark secret
whispered
many times in my life
and never understood.

Daughter of Adam

a detail from "The Legend of the True Cross" by Piero della Francesca

Piero painted me standing by
while dying Father Adam
requests the holy oil.

My skin is milk,
my eyes two dark plums
innocent yet of my body's call.

I am not looking at Father,
nor at the young man
whose gaze is open and alert.

My thoughts do not allow a glance
at the dark scene unfolding
the planting of seeds into my father's mouth,

the seeds of the tree whose sturdiness
will bear the weight of Holiness.
I will bear my own cross

budding now in my pink breast.

Fig Gathering

Suddenly
we stopped the car,
scrambled down
the gravelly hill

risking bloody knees,
the shine on city shoes.
Impatient to stain
the white of summer shirts,

we liberated the tongue,
stretched hands into the green heaven
picking the plumpest, the ready-to-split ones—
the lavish gift of a sultan.

Oozing pulp into the mouth
we ate the hearts of a thousand trees.
And then, after this solemn sinning,
we mopped our chins.

On such a day as this the world came into being.

Anogi

Ithaca, 2010

Wind all night whistling
through the ruins
left by the earthquake in 1953.

We arrived only days ago
to find seclusion
at the top of a mountain.

Why, we wondered,
had they not cleared
away the rubble?

Outside: stacks of grey stone
thickets of thistles
to torment all but the goats.

Inside: yellow wooden table
wildflowers in a glass
oil lamp, which we lit to read

of Homer's wine-sodden sailor
falling off the roof
when roused in the night to service.

Those things happen—
falling off the roof
in the middle of the night

or into a crevice of the earth.
George tells of the earthquake,
how the earth beneath them

let out a deep groan,
which entered his body
and has never left it—

like an uninvited spirit
grown familiar—
and accommodated.

Florentine Extravagance

Today it rained.
It thundered and clacked
like the devil.

Did we care?
We bought a red umbrella
linked arms to hold it

then paraded across the piazza
our elegant Italian shoes
squeaking dripping slipping

into puddle mouths
while the rest of Florence
huddled together

in front of shop doors—
astonished at the sight
of such extravagance.

Immanence

Today I visited the famous Uffizi.
This was my fifth climb
up the ducal staircase
leading to the Renaissance.

On the way to Botticelli
Giotto called me to his side.
His troubled Boy
looked darkly towards the future.

Mary sat in peace
blue velvet cloak
around her shoulders
breasts shining tender
slender fingers clasping beauty—
her gaze on me.

Masaccio, Fra Angelico,
Botticelli, Michelangelo—
they all knew
Giotto had discovered
the human in paint.

It has taken me
five centuries and
five climbs.

Turquoise is French

I
Turquoise is French—
though she slept first in ancient Persian mines,
then, like a queen, was gently roused and carried
swathed in veils on the backs of camels.
The route to France lay *à travers Turquie*.
Bearing the name of its passage—
la pierre turquoise—
she crossed deserts, mountains,
a treacherous sea.

II
Ah, my love,
hydrated phosphate of copper and aluminum,
you nest between fruitful green and
fluent blue.
In arias with red
you sing the highs and lows
in every register of love.
You bring harmony to the home
talk depression off the ledge.

III
You are French for *voulez-vous*
for desire in the heart and head
for the green-blue waters of love
for deep mines, hot sands, red suns
for never-ending journeys on camels' backs
for wild mayhem, my love
for kissing, touching—
turquoising, my love—
I have come for you, my queen.

At Casa Letizia

Lerici, Italy

At 5:30 this morning,
with skill and flutter,
the doves began their
ancient abracadabra.

It worked because
the sky began to pinken.

The puritan moon sat still,
in a remnant of gray,
three quarters of the way
to being whole.

Whole, quarters, full—
what do words mean?
Still
the moon moves oceans,
the dove pulls magic
out of its heart.

None Too Early

He came to me last night
in a dream—
my French boyfriend
from that cobblestone-throwing
decade past
not stooped as he is now
white-haired and rickety

but as he was when I was twenty
when I admired his hair fine as spider silk
his pressed raincoat
his polished shoes
when I found the second taste
of Gauloises near divine
taken from the halo of his mouth.

There he was in dream flesh
after fifty years of lying low.
I asked *Want a drink?*
Glancing at his watch he said
Too early—laying down
the law in the French way.

But lawless moments
were once the rule.
This has taken all my life
to understand.

Waves

I remember you on the beach at Manasquan,
    for throwing me under like a threshing
        wheel.

My body tumbled into the salted underworld
    pulled into the current like a lost sack of
        jewels.

I am sure my heart was kicking,
    but no thought of that. I wanted one thing:
        breath.

When I surfaced, teeth, hair, skin,
    slaked with salt, I stumbled to shore.
        Love

Is like that, the body an ocean
    tumbling ships like playthings off its wild
        edges.

To the Tango Shoe

strappy black
red-rosetted
leather-soled
free-souled
sex on a stick

slinking up
slinking down
kicking flicking
in fine fabulation

dance me high
dance me low
real low baby

you foot-kisser of hot romance
burn a hole
and smoke out the devil

sweep and swivel
steam and sizzle
like a subway train

take me where
I want to go,
you know,
Shoe—

away from here

The death of the fly

in a Venus flytrap is unpeaceful,
like any caused by a fatal wooing.

The fly's legs protruding
from the plant's fibrous teeth

dance like fallen Rockettes
heaped higgledy-piggledy.

But wonder is my theme—
not death. Wonder—

that furious life exists
in delicate limbs, each the breadth

of a hair on a newborn's head.

Diagnosis for Back Pain

I hobbled,
bent like a hairpin
a cripple in her prime.

X-rays revealed not only
a curved spinal
xylophone

but a dozen mini-
musicians
with tiny wooden mallets.

Ultrasound captured
their vertiginous music—
strange bone-rattling sounds.

Despite the inconvenience
of twelve obsessive music-makers
boarding at my expense,

I might have been happy.
I was a medical wonder.
But then the little suckers

wanted variations on a theme,
added a string section,
began picking and plucking

my fine taut nerves.
That's when I doubled
over and screamed.

They thought I didn't
like their music,
that I was square.

I didn't care. Anyway,
it was their last gig together.
Mr. Sawbones saw to that.

Compromised

part feather
part knife

part whisper
part bullet

part dirty French post card
part sweet freesia

part caress
part stranglehold

part flower
part sewer

it is not enough to punish
it is not enough to forgive

locked as we are
in the pith of pine.

The Middle Way

I'll tell you how I found the middle way:
By loving those who scrape their backs on knives,
First one side of duality, then the other.

Finding enough bandages was exhausting,
Running here and there was bloody work,
So—I stood in the middle and sang.

I'll tell you how I found the middle way:
By loving those who did not bandage my back,
They suffered me to live with self-infliction.

This I considered somewhat cruel.
Where was the pity due me? But all at once,
I heard music; I stopped in the middle and listened.

North Truro

In muggy sea air
the chirr of Cape crickets
is ragged and loud.
It's been another night of
triumphal mating.

The Big Dipper above
cups the sound like
rare moon water—
those old cold stars
jealous of earthly warmth.

Here I Am

To radiant light I woke. Not a vision
but a shining moon ribboning light
upon my face. I would rather have had a legion
of angels staring down upon the sight
of me, human, restless with human questions.
But as it was, I took what was given
and allowed the importuning moon its best run
of seduction. Lying in bed, kindled
by desire, I watched the classic show:
Cynthia behind a cloud-screen darkly sooty—
now hiding in white wisps of vaporous flow—
then dropping all in brazen beauty.
If seduction is all we have of knowable splendor,
then here I am, World.

Joan of Arc and the Angels

after the painting by Jules Bastien-Lepage

Joan stands
outside her father's cottage
in shades of green, rustic gold,
brown, which is her humility,
which is the color of her tattered skirt—
full for striding in the furrows.

A loosely-laced bodice
covers a rough undergarment;
she has gathered and shaped her hair
like bread at the nape of her neck,
her limpid eyes
unseeing of this world.

She is listening and
will soon turn to find
floating like vapors over the morning fields:
gold-armored Michael
with a silver sword,
St. Margaret, St. Catherine,
diaphanously white
wreathed in flowers.

Go, daughter of God.
Raise an army.
Drive out the English.
Crown the dauphin King.

We are told she began to weep,
not for the impossible task—
but for the beauty of angels.

Revisiting Orvieto

Spring 1348

I should tell you that
I am a peasant
that I have no shoes
that I prayed to St. Raphael
to heal my dying mother.

You will be surprised
that I walked with dirty feet
up to the holy sanctuary
bent my scabby knees
to offer a small song, a small prayer.

No one heard
but my saint—
not even the lurking priest
who thought I was there
to steal the candles.

Then I returned from the church
along sunbaked cobbles
(to this day I hate cobbles)
to the outdoor bed
that I had made for my mother—

outdoor so she could see heaven
for as long as she could hold the blue sky
with her green eyes though the seeing hurt.
Also, it was easier to wash away
the leavings from her body.

She died that day—
and since I had no money
the nuns of the town wrapped her body
in a shroud clean and fresh-smelling like lavender
the best wrapping she'd ever had—

lowered her quickly into a grave
with all the others who had died fevered
with swollen lumps of flesh under their arms.
At twilight I returned to offer a song, a prayer.
No one heard but my saint.

Polina & the Pomegranate

When the hammer and sickle
no longer topped the Kremlin
she came to visit
had packed a snack
hidden in her handbag
asked if she could eat it
though I'd offered cake.

After slipping on a thin pair of rubber gloves
over her still girl-like hands
she quartered the pomegranate
scooped up the seedy pulp with a spoon
hunched over the plate and ate
alert, ravenous
like a dog jealous of its bone.

What I learned was this:
she grew up starving.
I say *grew* but not much.
She'd made good in a traveling circus
limbs just the size to be flashed from a cannon
hired for nothing but food
she a tender spoon of flesh.

Abridgment

When I married in my twenties, the mountain
sky was blue, my home-sewn dress long & white

somehow I was forty, the sky was black thunder—
and lightning struck my lips, and for many seasons

there was no weather, no night or day, and
now I am seventy and my prayers have changed

from bending the knee to bowing the head—
and again there is mountain, sky, around me

rising from the dark knots of the city
and the doors of decades are open.

Through them pour
all the fleeting days of my life.

Bon Art

You attracted me,
Bonnard,
years ago when I stood

light, innocent,
and you, naked,
bathed in color.

I find you again—
in purples, blues,
stripped and splashing.

Oh. Oh.
Invigorating
to a body gone to gravity.

Private Map

Haunches. Two round melons—
the split between usually out of sight.
What fills out jeans.
What stretches to the breaking point
your moisture-wicking bib shorts.

You remember that stoney list
of chisel-resistant descriptors:
hefty, generous, zaftig
while you, who always wears dresses
to keep the twins in one stroller,
dream of the slender honey dews

of a bone-rich enchantress
who swirls her evening kale juice
with a crystal stick
who worships at the barre,
not in roomy easy chairs as do you.

Ah! sweet consolation—
your private map of woman spread
marks a movable Massif Central,
appreciated for its natural environment,
its rivers and mountains,
its surprising wildlife, and in the end,
its steadying presence.

Pink Feathers

for Saundra Buys

For me, pink feathers do not
connote flamingoes
or campy cabaret singers.

Pink feathers point me to
this female body-house that
I have house-kept for seventy years—

this because a physician-in-training
once described her experience
of dissecting a female body,

gently probing
the finger-like projections
on the end of fallopian tubes.

They were like
pink feathers, she said
the fimbriae—

used efficiently every month
to sweep the ovum
into the waiting room.

No need now to keep
the house tidy, but the flamingoes
still preen in pink feather scarves.

Irish Peat

The Burren, 2003

This morning when I woke
I tried to remember the poem
I'd written in my head last night
before falling asleep.
I tried to remember by naming
all the poems I might have written—

about the black shine of flagstones around the hearth
or the pebbly sores in my mouth from the sugar in my tea
or that grey strip of clouds rimming the sky
perhaps the magic in the marbled-brown of a hazel stick.

Or was the poem about the stone beds of saints
or the earthy warmth of my feather duvet?
Perhaps a wish for a bright knit scarf
because I had come gravely, all in black.

My mind somersaulted in memory:
a man kissing my hand, then kissing it again
the farmer-prophet proclaiming at the dappled spring
a friend embroidering in the sun
an old dog shaking his rabbit prey

sheets of limestone erupting like monstrous bones
scatterings of small flowers:
wild geraniums, primroses
native orchids on tiny stiff stems
one delicate gentian.

These were not the poem.
I only remember my dream:
each soul lay as a brick of ancient peat
stretched end to end in a vast, smoking circle—
each catching fire from its neighbor
this morning when I woke.

Sitting with the Quakers

A weakened sun streamed
through cloudy panes,
tingeing with light
the floor's irregular stony flags.

Straight-backed pews circled the table,
its rough-hewn legs hemmed
with a square of planks
braced for another century of service.

Suddenly, scurrying out of hiding,
a feverish shrew darted
about the perimeter,
shot a path between two black shoes

of an undisturbed Quaker.
Oh, to be less the runner
and more the sitter,
seeing.

Harsh Winter

Let us go into the white forest
gather white flowers—
winter berries and snowdrops
dressed in fragility.

Let us go into the white forest
gather white flowers—
though our hearts are red
our eyes, our hands are red.

In Entire Forgetfulness

We wake to weak morning light
in entire forgetfulness.

There is order everywhere—
except here, in the head,

which even in dreams
spins us into misrule

without light
to keep the lines.

A miracle has occurred.
Once more the sun has burned

the midnight oil,
kept watch while we slept.

We have not reeled off
into the void.

In-between Time

Last night,
when a single star
lit the sky,
I opened the door
to a world without time.

Nothing moved—
not a single leaf
on the ten-thousand-leafed
sycamore guarding the gate
these hundred years.

The thick grass
of close-lying fields—
a luminous glass ocean,
barn owl silent, fox appeased,
hare at rest in the nesting dark.

It was only a moment,
of white star on black sky.

Night Sky

The moon is covered with haze tonight, filmy
like the scrim on a stage;
I long to see beyond the striations moving
like sea foam.

What can this world mean
if sight is never given?
The moon lies 239 thousand miles away
once wished on like a genie's lamp
now held in the hand
like the common basalt it is.

I said to the blackbird singing in the hedge,

you sweet vaudevillian
you sleek feathered creature with
the golden beak
you bringer of night song
I am listening.

The clouds part. The moon
is a spotlight spotting me
as I spot its cratered surface
struck with eons of
meteorites.

I am pulled into its sphere.

I feel
my own cratered
sleeping self.

Look, haven't I always known
I am the moon?
I am the moon rising
from my belly to my eyes.

Look,
I want to be not me, not the moon, the myth
not mineral, bird, crater, cloud,
nothing in particular, seen or unseen.
It is the I am I am after
the I am after death
the I am before I am born.

The Egyptian Water Lily

Its petals are blue.

It once dressed
the bodies of pharaohs
and put the lotus-eaters
into ecstatic sleep,
a cerulean blue—
the sky of water.

And like the sky
it bursts and scatters
when the pod brims full—
like us, our tears brimming
in the dark eye of pond.

Galaxies

When a child toes her first cold wave,
When you observe a beetle burrowing into antique bark
When you smell newly-flurried pastures
When the courtesan's courtiers vanish
When the water flows again from the rusting pump
When your life is a cloud of burning ash
When the bin man finds your wallet
When the programmer discovers out-of-bound bugs
When the body loves the wilderness it is lost in
Here is the mind spinning into deep time.

Open Studio

The canvas of day is painted
with sound.

One stroke, then silence.
Then one more.

A bird. A whistle of wind.

What hand is painting?

That signature—
the same and different.

Same and different.

Let me see to the end
of this mystery.

Matinee

This afternoon
I'm attending
the ballet.

Program: Creation.
Music: Wind
Principal Dancers: Trees

Limbs only express
the terror—

they quiver and shake
bend and bow
fling about in frenzy—

not knowing the steps
only the dance.

Metaphor

Once, a cow in the field beside our cottage
cried loudly all night long
for her missing calf.

Let me be perfectly clear.
The field was Time.
The cry was Mine.

No Mind at Howk Waterfall

Caldbeck, Cumbria

I had killed a graceful creature,
left it for roadkill.
Singing at the top of my lungs
while rounding the hedgerow,
I had not seen it coming loose
from the landscape.

Now I stood on the narrow footbridge,
drinking in the fizz of negative ions
scattered by the tumbling water.
So deafening was the sound
so deep the ravine,
for a moment: blackout—

no reason, no waterfall
no bounding deer in the mind.

432 Hz

everything is vibration
every thing
sings
wind sings
fire sings
rocks sing
hard unmoving
rocks
singing
for millions of years
in waves
like water

To the Poet Offering an Opinion on the Rapture

> *"The evaporation of the 4 million who believe this crap would leave the world an instantly better place."*
> *—NPR, December 19, 1995*

I have only this to say:

All we have for world
is belief and its negation.
We, knee-deep in creation,
cannot spin without holes:
the ruly and unruly
light and its shards.
We stand intricately connected
to the wholly abandoned.

Philip Glass Concert

aging fingers on piano
music born
without age

right holding line
of melody
left the eternal wave.

ear hears
mind stills
heart opens

Drumbeat

Listen to the heart,
the poet said,
or you will end up bitter—
and bitter is
beyond even grief.

Heart, I've stretched you
taut like a goat skin,
have carried you
for seventy years
within my chest
strapped on a thong
of kikuyu leaves.

I have heard the beating:
de-sire de-sire.
My death will be
sweet.

On My Seventieth Birthday

The potato skins pile up in the sink.
I flick the sharp edge again and again
weighing the breasty heft in my hand
smelling its watery sweet-milk scent.
Someone, something dug it up
from its months-long incubation.
Did the harvester wait until the leaves
had yellowed? Had the skin matured
into tender-tough resistance?
I reach into the tangled mesh
two potatoes, one potato, then no more—
grateful to come to the end of my task.

Wind

The small room is suddenly alive with a moan
whistling through the old panes—
a groan and a rattle, fierce and low

when the wind blows frigid from the river—
more Arctic than we would think
in the hot glitter of the city—

wailing, menacing, and heard by the many
huddled in apartments by their loose windows
and overworked radiators.

The wind speaks an otherworldly tongue
to anyone with ears, not just to little ones
or to old ones prone to nervous fright.

Is there only fragile glass between us and this—
which is howling our name
and the names of eight million more?

On Finding a Deliquescing Mouse in the Bathtub Drain

> *"Nearly all the elements in the human body were made in a star and many have come through several supernovas." —Dr. Ashley King, Planetary Scientist and Stardust Expert, Natural History Museum*

As soon as the door is locked
rooms fill with emptiness
although everything remains:
chairs, table, books
every thing
exactly where we left them.

In a locked house
there's no explaining stillness
amid constant shifting:
curtains fading
dust swirling
the house plant unfurling its one pale green leaf
all the scurrying, burrowing creatures
I have no eyes to see.
So it was that I locked the cottage—
left it still but moving for three months.

When did the mouse fall into the tub?
It must have tried scampering
up the slippery porcelain's sides many times
until, in exhaustion, it settled flesh and bone
into the small round hole
as we all will do thinking it's over
when there is still movement to be undergone
from solid into liquid into gas
and after eons of time
into another star.

Weight

Stay by my side, poet shadow,
while the thunder grumbles
in its faraway place.
I step lightly into the boat.
Yet the weight
  is mortal.
Even the water knows this.
The journey across
  will be momentous.

Washing the Dead

I have washed the dead before.
Where's the wonder in that?

Have you never combed the hair
of the beloved?
Slipped an arm into a sleeve?

Dead, whatever it means,
has never meant
love is no more.

Elemental Alchemy

The effort it takes to die
will make magicians
of us all.

I thought he was getting better
said the daughter.
He sat up and ate a biscuit—

when what she witnessed
was her father summoning skill
from his now frayed black hat,

he the alchemist
transmuting the lead of bone
into light.

Seeing the Last

I've always wondered why
if you know you're about to die
you don't close your eyes.

Isn't this the big sleep?
And we all know it's not polite to stare—
although maybe I'll want to see

until the very last moment—
my eyes on this world—

my eyes on the beloved
as I descend or ascend
into night or light.

Close my eyes then,
orchestrator of my life,
with a soft downward stroke,

when I've seen my last
of you, my love.

Kathryn Kimball grew up in Montgomery, Alabama, has a Ph.D. in English Literature, and taught writing and nineteenth-century British and American literature. She divides her time between New York City and Carlisle, Cumbria, and has been a yoga practitioner for thirty years. Her published work includes a 2021 chapbook and various poems and French poetry translations in literary journals. She won the *Columbia Journal*'s 2023 prize for translation.

www.ingramcontent.com/pod-product-compliance
Lightning Source LLC
Chambersburg PA
CBHW030059170426
43197CB00010B/1592